ICE HOCKEY

Ronald Litke

First published in Great Britain by Heinemann Library
Halley Court, Jordan Hill, Oxford, OX2 8EJ
a division of Reed Educational & Professional Publishing Ltd

OXFORD FLORENCE PRAGUE MADRID ATHENS
MELBOURNE AUCKLAND KUALA LUMPUR SINGAPORE TOKYO
IBADAN NAIROBI KAMPALA JOHANNESBURG GABORONE
PORTSMOUTH NH (USA) CHICAGO MEXICO CITY SAO PAULO

Printed in the United States of America by Lake Book
Manufacturing, Inc.

00 99 98 97 96
10 9 8 7 6 5 4 3 2 1

ISBN 0 431 07429 1

British Library Cataloguing in Publication Data
Litke, Ronald.
    Ice Hockey. – (Successful sports)
    1. Hockey – Juvenile literature.
    I. Title.
    796.9'62

Acknowledgments
The publishers would like to thank the following for
permission to reproduce phtotgraphs:
Allsport USA/Glenn Cratty: pp. 1, 22; Allsport
USA/Harry Scull: p. 25; AP/Wide World Photos/Bob
Galbraith: p. 5; B. Bennett Studios/©Bruce Bennett:
pp. 10, 18, 26; B. Bennett Studios/©Scott Levy: p. 12;
Dave Black: pp. 8, 16, 20; Duomo/William R. Sallaz:
p. 2; Duomo/Paul J. Sutton: p. 27; Focus on Sports: p.
13; Focus on Sports/Jerry Wachter: p. 19; Hockey Hall
of Fame Archives: p. 28; Hockey Hall of Fame
Archives/Doug MacLellan: front cover; David
Madison: pp. 11, 14; (Rigby/UK): p. 23; Sports Photo
Masters/©Don Smith: pp. 9, 29; UPI Bettmann: p. 24;

Illustrators: Stephen Brayfield: p. 7; Robert Voigts

Our thanks to David Pickles, Secretary of the British
Ice Hockey Association, for his comments in the
preparation of this book.

The front cover photo shows Wayne Gretsky.

The title page photo shows Mario Lemieux of the
Pittsburgh Penguins.

Contents

Introduction

Ice hockey is the fastest team sport. There is nothing quite like the sensation of moving at great speed with the **puck** on your **stick** and the determination to score – unless it's making a great pass to set up a team-mate for a goal or helping your **goalie** to stop a shot reaching the net. Ice hockey combines all the great dramatic moments and techniques of team sports, but with one significant difference – the playing surface. Ice makes the game fast and fluid. The action moves back and forth in seconds, and the direction of the puck does the same. That's why the game is so exciting to play and to watch.

While it is difficult to trace the exact beginnings of hockey, the game is thought to be invented in the 1850s by British soldiers on the frozen rivers of Canada. It was first played seriously in this country in the 1930s, though its origins date back to the turn of the century. In North America, the first major organized league was formed in the 1890s and known as the National Hockey Association of Canada Limited. There were two teams in Montreal – the Canadiens and Wanderers – and the Ottawa Senators and the Quebec Bulldogs.

HOCKEY FACTS

Fair Play trophies are awarded by many leagues in Europe. They are often sponsored by manufacturers or big companies. They are awarded to the team or player who records the fewest penalty minutes.

Not very much has changed since then. It's still sticks and skates, five on five (with a goalie for each team) and the hard rubber disk, the puck. The game in Great Britain has now expanded to two major national senior leagues – English and Scottish leagues – with teams from Northern Ireland and Wales involved. There are also junior leagues at under 10, 12, 14, 16 and 19 years and a women's league. There are now over 8000 registered players in Great Britain with a 15 per cent increase in playing numbers every season.

The popularity of ice hockey comes from the joy of skating, the thrill of competition and the satisfaction of playing with a team. Also, because it is played on ice, the skill of hockey depends more on the ability to skate – which can be learned – rather than on strength or height, which cannot.

Wayne Gretzky of the Los Angeles Kings never stopped practising. His father once told him, 'Wayne, keep practising and one day you're gonna have so many trophies, we're not gonna have room for them all.' His father was right.

Gordie Howe and Wayne Gretzky, perhaps the two greatest professional ice hockey players of all time.

Goals of the game

Although the equipment has improved and changed in looks, ice hockey is still a basic sport. The purposes of the **stick**, skates, and pads are still the same as always. It's how you use the equipment that makes the difference. Of course, sports is about ability, but it also takes thought and preparation, learning and practice. Because the action of an ice hockey game is so fast, there is no time to make up shots, or for a player to try to win alone. Ice hockey is more fun, and winning is more satisfying, when the team works together. That's how the professionals do it.

Count on coaches

As good as professionals are, they still listen to their coach. The Sheffield Steelers, Britain's most successful team, consider their coach to be the most important member of the team. The coach can see what each player does best. That means the coach can combine the talent of all the players to create offensive lines that can score, quick and able defence pairs that help the **goalies** and a good team spirit.

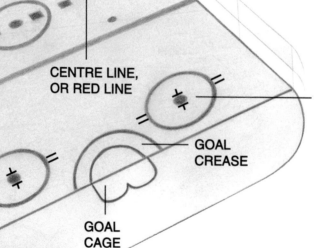

CENTRE LINE, OR RED LINE

END ZONE FACE-OFF SPOT AND CIRCLE

GOAL CREASE

GOAL CAGE

Ice hockey rinks vary in size, with European rinks generally longer than American rinks.

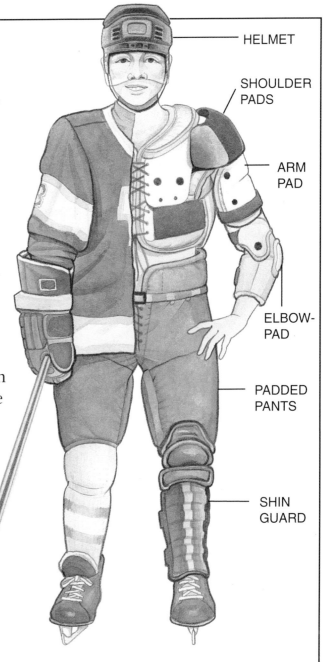

HELMET

SHOULDER PADS

ARM PAD

ELBOW-PAD

PADDED PANTS

SHIN GUARD

It's always best to have full equipment to play ice hockey. This includes pads for vunerable areas at high-risk for injury, such as the knees and the midsection – and, of course, a helmet.

Get ready to play

If you're interested in playing hockey, it may take a long time before you actually join a team. You need time to learn how to skate, practise the basics, get in condition, and find out what your skills are and what position you want to play. Each position in ice hockey contributes equally to the success of the team. While many of the most popular players are the offensive **centres** and **wings** who score goals, the true heroes are playing defence. No matter how good the offence might be, if the other team scores more goals your team will lose. As with most sports, it is defence that really wins games.

The great professional ice hockey teams have a balance of good offence and defence. Players from different positions help out all over the rink and adjust to each other as the conditions of the game change. A team must be as good **playing short-handed** as it is on the **power play**, when it has an advantage.

Before you begin to play ice hockey, decide what your goals will be as a player. These early decisions will go a long way towards your success.

Pointers

If you're thinking about playing ice hockey, talk about it with your friends, parents and coaches. You need their advice and support to make the right decision.

Skills in skating

As reading is to learning, skating is to ice hockey. It is fundamental. It is the most important skill to learn. If you can skate well, you can play any position and greatly extend the range of that position. Because players now skate better and faster than ever, they are expected to be able to roam the ice and help out where needed. Even **goalies** extend their range by passing and **clearing** the **puck** from the defending zone. They cannot do this if they do not skate well. The basic skills of skating include the following.

The forward stride

Start with legs shoulder-width apart for balance. Bend the knees for comfort. Lean slightly forwards and bring your body closer to the ice for stability. Push forwards and downwards, off the back leg, moving forwards with the leg closer to the direction you want to go. Repeat, but with the other foot. Lift the legs just high enough for your skates to clear the ice. This prepares you for the next stride. Practise often – without a **stick** or other equipment first – and your speed will soon increase. Then try it with equipment.

The stop

Off the forward stride, try to stop by quickly turning your body (and your skates) at a right angle and, with knees bent and feet still shoulder-width apart, pressing both skates hard into the ice. Try not to favour one leg, because both are needed to stop. Practise this on both sides.

Skating backwards

Stand with knees bent, shoulder-width apart, as if you are just about to lower yourself into a chair. Then slowly move your hips from side to side, bending slightly forwards and pushing backwards towards your toes at the same time. This motion will force you backwards. You can move further to the left and right by pushing on the inside edge of the right skate (to go left) and the inside edge of the left skate (to go right). Your speed will increase as the motion becomes more smooth and you feel more confident.

Even after you feel comfortable with a skill, try it again, only faster. Always remember, practice makes perfect.

Pointers

The crossover is best practised by tracing the number 8 into the ice. After each forward stride, one skate is crossed over the other to make the direction change. Doing this will help you become nimble enough to cross over to the left and right sides.

The *crossover* is the most important skill in skating. When done properly, it allows you to change direction quickly, and turn a curve around the net, either forwards or backwards, without losing speed or balance.

Planning to practise

There are many levels of practice for anyone who wants to become a complete ice hockey player. You should always try to make time to practise. Even if you cannot get to a rink, there are other ways to practise. Many ice hockey coaches suggest that their players also learn ballet to learn about balance and movement.

If you can get to a rink, practise your skating skills. Work with the **stick** to learn how to move the **puck** and to pass it to team-mates. It's best to practise with a coach; however, this is not always possible. Often you have to teach yourself and learn with friends or family.

Pointers

Your pre-game meal should be eaten no later than three to four hours before game time. This allows your body to digest the food properly for energy storage. Fruits, cereals, and grains – including pasta – washed down with two or three glasses of milk or water are ideal choices.

Crisp, accurate passing takes many hours of practice to learn the correct timing.

Equipment basics

Your equipment must fit properly. Your stick should have a **lie** – the angle between the blade and handle – that is comfortable for you. This will allow you to handle the puck more effectively. The cuffs of your gloves should cover your forearms for protection. Your shin pads must be strong but flexible. Your trousers must have pads for your thighs and midsection, but they should not be bulky. Your shoulder pads should fit snugly but should allow your arms to move. Remember, don't ever practise or play without a helmet and a mouthguard.

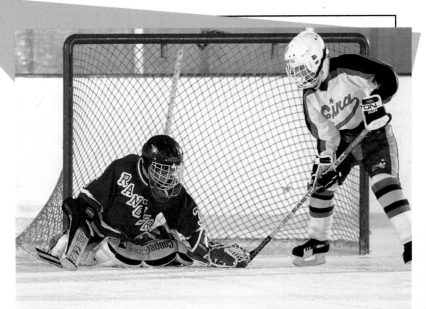

Practising techniques

When you practise by yourself, spend lots of time doing skating drills (with and without a stick and puck), stickhandling with the puck, trying various shots, and passing toward targets for different lengths and angles, from a standing position and while moving. This routine will allow you to build your skills in the right order to become a complete player.

When you practise with friends, switch positions from offence to defence and from giving to receiving passes. It is also a good idea to race. This helps to make the skating drills, such as **crossovers**, skating backwards and stopping in the shortest distance, even more challenging. If you have the proper equipment, take turns at being **goalie**. This helps you get over any fear of the puck, no matter how fast it comes at you.

Practising ice hockey is like learning anything else. It only looks difficult if you are inexperienced.

It's helpful to learn all the positions. If you can get the equipment, take turns with your friends playing goalie. This will make you a well-rounded player and give you a better understanding of the game.

Shots that score

There are a lot of shots in ice hockey. Using them effectively involves much more than strength – accuracy is just as important as power. During an actual game, even the best players may not get more than four or five chances to shoot at the goal, so it is important to make the most of every opportunity.

The actual power behind shots is not really in the arms. Learning how to transfer your weight from the back foot to the front foot at the right moment – using your entire body – is what gives any shot its power.

The key shots in hockey include the following:

The forehand wrist shot

This is the most common shot in ice hockey and is possibly the most accurate. The wrist shot is a great shot from anywhere from 10 to 40 feet (3–13 metres) away from the goal. Begin this shot by positioning yourself and the **stick** at right angles to the **puck**. Then, placing the puck at the heel of the stick, start a sweeping motion, transferring your weight from your back leg to your front leg. Turn your wrists over hard just as your weight shifts, keeping the puck on the stick until the last moment. Follow through completely, bringing your back leg up for balance. Your follow-through will determine your accuracy. Practise this shot first while standing still, then while moving forwards.

The wrist shot is the most versatile shot. With a quick thrust of the wrists forward, you can make the puck travel low, fast, and accurately. The wrist shot is a hard shot to stop.

Pointers

When practising ice hockey, examine the type of play with which you feel most competitive. Many players who like the speed of hockey want to chase the puck wherever it goes. Others like to watch the play in front of them and choose their opportunities – whether to score or to break up an opponent's play.

The slap shot

Everyone wants to be good at this shot, but it takes practice. Position yourself and the stick at right angles to the puck. Bring the stick backwards to about waist level (keeping the blade turned down), then shift your weight from your back leg to your front leg. The point of impact (aim just behind the puck) comes just as you reach the middle of the swing. Then follow through. This shot will also causes your back leg to lift for balance.

The backhand shot

Though not as powerful as forehand shots, backhands are still very accurate – and they allow you to lift the puck over the **goalie's** pads or stick. There are several kinds of backhand that are actually just different forms of the forehand wrist shot. By simply reversing the motion of the forehand, you can sweep a backhand (the motion feels more like pulling), or simply snap your wrists for a quick flick at the goal.

The slap shot is best practised by lining up a series of pucks and hitting each one to a different spot in the net. By changing the speed and depth of your wind-up, you can develop great accuracy.

Picking your position

I ce hockey may look like a free-flowing and unorganized game, because the action is so fast. Unlike football or baseball – but a lot like basketball – ice hockey allows its players to roam all over the playing surface but they still keep their assigned responsibilities. When considering a position to play, think about what best suits your abilities and range.

Offensive players have several key responsibilities. These include setting up plays, **forechecking**, passing, scoring, and helping out on defence. These tasks require strong skating ability and endurance, because offensive players make the most sudden changes of direction.

Playing defence needs an understanding of the tougher parts of the game, such as **digging** for the **puck**, blocking shots, and having a lot of body contact. Being a **goalie** is similar to being a catcher in baseball. The goalie is often the team leader, because that position requires someone who takes the greatest responsibility – stopping the other team from scoring. Every position has its rewards.

As ice hockey has evolved, several players have changed the way people think about certain positions and how to play the game. Jean Beliveau, the great **centre** of the Montreal Canadiens (1951–71), could start up the offence from inside his own defending zone by helping to pick away the puck from the other team's offence. In the 1985–86 season, Edmonton Oilers' defenceman Paul Coffey, who later joined the Detroit Red Wings, set a record by scoring 48 goals. He is able to handle his defensive responsibilities and contribute offensively. Coffey is also second best at **assists** among active players, with 934, behind only Wayne Gretzky.

On the other hand, fans today appreciate good defence. One of professional ice hockey's greatest players, Ken Dryden, rewrote the record book for goalies in the 1970s. He led the Canadiens to six **Stanley Cup** championships in only eight years. He also earned the **Vezina Trophy**, the award for the best goalkeeper, five times. A great defensive player can turn an entire team around. When Pierre Pilote joined the Chicago Blackhawks in the 1955–56 season, the team steadily improved in the standings and won the Stanley Cup only four seasons later.

HOCKEY FACTS

Professional ice hockey has two halls of fame. The Hockey Hall of Fame in Toronto, Canada, established in 1943, includes not only players but also referees, linesmen, owners and reporters. The United States Hockey Hall of Fame in Eveleth, Minnesota, opened in 1973 and also includes players, coaches and other people involved in the sport.

This Olympic match between the United States and Czechoslovakia shows the opening formation of players: the centre, the left wing, the right wing, the left and right defenders, and the goalie.

Remembering the rules

Ice hockey is definitely a contact sport, but the best players are those who observe the rules and play instead of fight. You won't see top players such as Tony Hand of the Sheffield Steelers or brothers Stephen Cooper of the Manchester Storm and Ian Cooper of the Cardiff Devils among the leaders in **penalty minutes**.

Some of the most exciting plays come from the face-off. In this play, the centre tries to draw the *puck* back to the right wing, who is positioned for a quick shot at the goal.

Penalties in hockey are severe. A player who is penalized must leave the ice, forcing their team to be **short-handed** for at least two minutes. During this time, the opposing team has a clear advantage to score.

The rules of ice hockey are not as complicated as those of American football or basketball. A professional game is 60 minutes long (three 20-minute periods). Junior games can range from 10 minutes to 15 minutes. Extra time varies with the type of league: in the professional league, it is a 10-minute 'sudden death' (when a goal ends the game), unless there is still a tie.

The main rules in ice hockey are **offside** rules. A team is ruled offside when a player passes the **puck** across two lines (red and blue). The other offside situation occurs when a player gets into the attacking zone before the puck does. When these plays are stopped, a **face-off** occurs either at the point of the penalty or outside the defending zone.

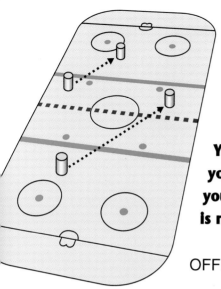

You will be called *offside* if you (a) pass the puck to a team-mate across two lines or (b) go across the blue line and into the attacking zone before the puck does.

You will be called for *icing* if, while playing defence, you shoot the puck from your half of the ice past your opponents' red goal line, and an opponent who is not the goalie touches it.

OFFSIDE

Icing is an illegal defensive play. Any time a defending player shoots the puck across three lines (centre, blue, and goal lines), 'icing' is called. The puck is then brought back for a face-off in the offensive team's end zone. Icing is most frequently used to stop an offensive attack, but the puck just comes straight back for the face-off.

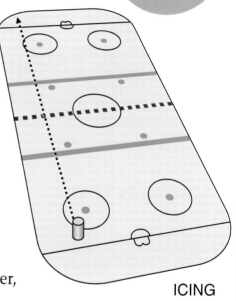

ICING

Sometimes penalties happen by accident; however, they can be prevented by following some simple suggestions:

• Don't hold onto another player or their **stick**.

• Don't trip another player in any way.

• Don't use your stick to stop a player in any way.

• Don't throw your body at an opponent.

Illegal plays such as holding, tripping, **hooking**, spearing, elbowing, **cross-checking** and fighting are generally used by players who are trying to make up for their lack of ability.

HOCKEY FACTS

The 1991–1992 NHL season saw many developments, including video replays to determine goals, the changing of the goal crease from a rectangle to a semicircle, and the disallowing of goals by any offensive player who stands on the goal crease line, is in the crease, or has a stick in the crease.

Getting in the game

There are many ice hockey teams for all ages, organized by local clubs and the English and Scottish Ice Hockey Associations. There are also teams in Wales and Northern Ireland. Whatever team you join, it is important to have an attitude that shows willingness to work for the benefit of the entire team.

Pointers

Nutrition is important no matter who you are. But athletes especially need extra calories. However, that does not mean they should eat 'junk food', which has large amounts of sugar, fat, or both. A balanced diet that includes whole grains, fruits, vegetables and white meat, such as chicken or turkey, is the sensible way.

Working with a coach

Becoming a good ice hockey player involves listening to the coach almost as much as playing the game. A good coach is patient but firm with players, offering criticism that does not hurt feelings but inspires players to perform better. In hockey you must learn the basic skills in the proper order if you want to become a complete player. The coach is your guide to learning those skills and to becoming a better player.

The goalie is usually the centre of attention in the game.

Understanding teamwork

The idea of teamwork is very important. No single player, no matter how good, can win a game alone. Successful teams find ways to combine individuals' strengths while limiting their weaknesses. The discipline of practising with a team will teach you to rely on your team-mates to help you, to give you a pass when you're **clear**, or to come back and support the defence.

When the Sheffield Steelers won the British League and Championship double in the 95–96 season, none of their players was in the list of UK top scorers, but as a unit they took some stopping. Their **goalie**, Martin McKay, let in fewer than four goals a game; legendary veteran defence player Chris Kelland, the ex-Great Britain captain, scored 68 league points; fellow defence players Ron Shudra, Rob Wilson and Mike O'Connor chipped in with over 150 points between them. The Steelers are the model for the modern ice hockey team. They did not fight much, but played aggressively with determination and skill.

Every team, no matter what level, develops its own style. The satisfaction gained in playing ice hockey does not always come from winning, but from playing your best. Some days, your team will come out on top. On others, it will be a different story. That's what makes competition so interesting.

Bobby Orr, who played for the Boston Bruins and Chicago Blackhawks (1966–79), was the first defence player to carry the puck like an offensive player. He changed the way defence players have played by expanding their range.

Opening the offence

There may be only three assigned offensive players, but today's hockey demands that every player – even the **goalie** – tries to score goals. The basic strategy of using a **centre** and two **wings** to score, with defensive players only to back them up, is no longer good enough.

Nowadays, the offence begins from wherever the team gets possession of the **puck**. A team's ability to convert from defence to offence – 'the transition game' – can open up a game quickly.

To be able to take advantage of scoring opportunities, a team has to be prepared with plays and has to be able to execute those plays with the right timing. For all this to happen, each player must understand their position on offence. The wings usually trail up and down the ice on the right or left side. Meanwhile, the centre roams the ice to get the puck and set up the wings. Sometimes, the wings approach the attacking zone straight ahead, and the centre waits for them to cut towards the goal for a pass.

A power play is possible when one team has more players on the ice than the other.

If they skate well, centres and wings can exchange positions by crossing in front of each other, confusing the defense with **drop** or **backhand passes** to set up clear shots. The more offensive players move *without the puck*, the better their chances of becoming clear for a shot.

The basic positioning for the offence is a triangle between the centre and wings. The defensive players position themselves at the top of the attacking zone. When the triangle of offensive players is spread properly, the other team's defence shouldn't be able to clog the passing lanes. Sometimes the offence is able to get in close or to push the puck back to a defensive player for a slap shot, or get a rebound off a save and score.

An offence is only successful when the whole team plays together. That means moving the puck around to the open player, or, if a player has the puck in good range, shooting it. Sometimes, offensive players may get checked or have to take some roughness from the defence while they're trying to score – but that's all part of the game.

Pointers

A good conditioning programme builds strength and develops the body and mind to meet the challenge of playing ice hockey. Ask your coach to help you design a programme.

In the *power play*, the offence takes advantage of the other team being shorthanded. Because there is more room in the attacking zone, players have the option to pass or move in, confusing the defence and moving closer towards the goal for a better shot.

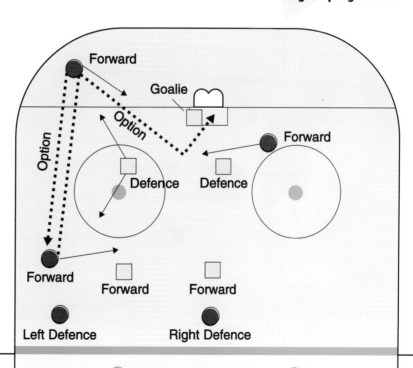

Durable defence

The most basic rule of defence is this: the **puck** may get past you, and the other player may get past you, but never let both past at the same time. Just as offence begins the moment a team gets possession of the puck, defence begins the moment a team loses the puck.

In defence, there are left and right positions as well as a **goalie**, but all six players on a team should be involved with defence. There are defensive plays, too. As in basketball, there can be **zone coverage**, where each player has a responsibility for a certain portion of the ice, or there can be one-on-one coverage. Because situations in ice hockey change so fast, one-on-one isn't always a reliable strategy.

A complete defensive strategy covers the whole ice. The first line of defence is actually the offensive players. They must **forecheck**, which means they must go into the opponent's defending or centre zone, chase down the player who has the puck and try to poke it away with different moves of their **sticks**. In such a situation, a defensive player could turn straight round and be on offence.

Chris Chelios of the Chicago Blackhawks is one of the finest all-around defence players in the NHL today. He combines a tough defence with the ability to assist and score goals.

Real defence takes place in the defending zone when the opponent is attacking. Defensive players are often the best skaters, because they change direction – backwards and forwards, left and right – more than the other players. Defensive players always try to position themselves between the offensive player and the goal.

Sometimes it may be necessary to **body-check** an opponent to prevent them from reaching the puck. In such cases, a player has to be sure to make contact. If contact is not made, the other player will get by. Checking is best accomplished by moving a shoulder or hip into the other player, staying low. After the check, the player gets back in the play by going for the puck or watching the goal.

The best defensive players are not afraid to try to block a shot with their sticks, skates or pads. To block a shot, a player must move in close to lessen the angle of the shot and either poke with the stick or move in front of the puck. A player can take the puck on the pads or skates. Blocking a goal can often be more important than scoring.

Here British teams Sheffield Steelers and Fife Flyers show one version of defending zone coverage. Tony Hand of the Steelers is shooting.

Pointers

Practise backward skating with players coming at you from your right and left sides. By doing this, you will develop defensive skills for both sides of the rink.

Guarding the goal

The **goalie** guards the smallest but most important space on the ice. Goalkeeping is one of the most difficult and challenging positions in sports. It requires concentration, speed while wearing heavy equipment, an ability to catch like a baseball player and fearlessness when a **puck** is speeding towards the goal.

Goalies are the only players who do not get a break during a game. No matter how intense any single play is, the goalie always has to be ready for another shot.

Although they are the last line of defence, goalies do not work alone. The defensive players must understand their responsibilities to the goalie and how they cover the area around the goal. The goalie must never be left alone when the opponent has the puck in the defending zone. If one defensive player goes into the corner to **dig** for the puck, the other should take position in front of the net.

Pointers

A goalie's skates are the best defense against low shots to the corners of the net. But to be effective, the goalie must keep his or her skate blade on the ice, or the puck may slip underneath.

Terry Sawchuk, who played with five teams in his 21-year career, leads all goalkeepers with 103 shutouts.

Communication between goalies and defensive players is essential. Goalies should constantly talk to defensive players. They can help them get to the right position or perhaps predict how an offensive play might be stopped before it becomes troublesome.

When all is said and done, it's up to the goalie to stop the shot. To do this, goalies have to remain standing as much as possible. Once a goalie's body is on the ice, the net is wide open. To narrow the chances for an offensive shot, the goalie should 'cut down the angle' of the shot. That is, the goalie should move towards the shooter to leave less room to shoot.

As much as possible, goalies should try to position their bodies centred on the puck, not the shooter. That gives the most chances – with body, **stick** and glove – to stop the shot.

Becoming a goalie takes hours of practice. Teams should line up a dozen pucks and have them shot quickly, in succession, with different types of shots and from different angles and points toward the goal. A goalie who can hold back this kind of attack is truly ready for the game.

Dominik Hasek of the Buffalo Sabres allowed only 1.95 goals per game in the 1993–94 season. That was the first time in 20 years that any goalie had an average under 2 goals per game.

Olympic glory

Some of the most exciting ice hockey games ever played have been during the Winter Olympics. Ice hockey was introduced to the Games in 1920 in Antwerp, Belgium, just after World War I. The Canadian team defeated the United States, Sweden, and Czechoslovakia to win the gold medal.

The 1920 Olympics were the beginning of Canada's domination of the sport through 1952. After that, the former Soviet Union (USSR) became a powerful team with a new style of strong skating, sharp passing, and quick shooting that changed the way ice hockey was played. Between 1956 and 1984, the Soviet Union played 52 games, winning 46 times with only four defeats and two ties.

The 1994 Olympic ice hockey gold medal was won by the Swedish hockey team. Its victory returned the style of international play to more passing and finesse.

The Soviet team's amazing run was broken only twice. The United States took the gold in 1960 and 1980, when the Games were in held in America. Both of these US teams were quite inexperienced. Fans worried they could not outplay the Soviets. But what the team lacked in talent, it made up for with enthusiasm and determination.

Pointers

To master ice hockey, it isn't enough just to play and watch. While playing helps to learn the discipline of practice and the meaning of teamwork, and watching hockey games can show you the result of all the hard work the professionals put in, reading can show you even more. Many professional players have written books that describe their techniques.

The 1980 series in Lake Placid, New York, was perhaps the US team's greatest. The team was ranked seventh before the Games began, but it came from behind in nearly every game to win the early rounds. The US coach, Herb Brooks, believed in discipline. The US team entered the gold-medal round with emotions running high.

It was surprising enough that the US team reached a 2–2 tie with Finland and earned a match with the USSR. The Soviets scored first, as expected, but the United States tied the game within five minutes. Only three minutes later, close to the end of the first period, the Soviets scored again. But the US team again tied the score on a **tip-in.**

The 1980 US hockey team won the gold medal in Lake Placid, New York, against long odds. Thus their nickname, the 'Miracle on Ice'.

The Soviets opened the second period with a **power play** goal and held a 3–2 lead into the final period. But at 8:39 of the third, US winger Mark Johnson poked the **puck** loose from a Soviet defender and scored. And only 1½ minutes later, US captain Mike Eruzione hit a slap shot past Soviet **goalie** Vladimir Myshkin for a 4–3 victory. The United States went on to win the gold by defeating Finland, 4–2, two days later.

Path to the pros

The British Ice Hockey leagues attract players from many different countries. Most of the foreign 'import' players come from Canada, but there are many Americans, plus players from all over Europe, including Finland, Sweden, Denmark, Holland, Romania, Lithuania and the Ukraine. There are also many EC passport holders with EC/Canadian citizenship, for example, Canadian Greeks and Italians.

The greatest number of players come from the Canadian leagues, such as the East Coast Hockey League and the International Hockey League. Some have had NHL experience, such as the legendary Doug Smail, who played 845 NHL games, and Gary Unger, who played over 1100 NHL games. Keith Gretsky, brother of the great Wayne Gretsky, also had a brief spell here.

Willie O'Ree was the first African-American player in the NHL, playing for the Boston Bruins for two seasons beginning in 1957.

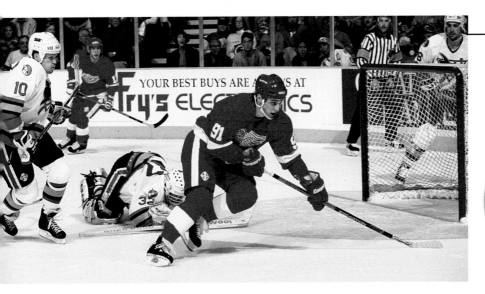

Players and coaches who wish to play here without EC nationality must obtain a work permit, just like other sports players or entertainers. There is a minimum level of work set by the Department of Employment, the British Ice Hockey Association and the Ice Hockey Players' Association. The restriction is to protect British-raised and developed players.

Whether you're set on becoming a professional player or just want to play for some competition and exercise, ice hockey is a game you can work at all your life. It's possible to improve your skating, shooting and other skills over many years.

For Wayne Gretzky of the Los Angeles Kings, his love of hockey started early and has not let up for 15 seasons. He says, 'I could skate at two. I was nationally known at six. I was signing autographs at ten… I turned pro and kept going to high school.' But Gretzky's father also told him not to become 'bigheaded'. The greatest player in the game still says the highest compliment is that he 'works hard every day'.

Sergei Federov, a centre for the Detroit Red Wings, was recruited from Russia. He is one of the NHL's top defensive forwards. His European style emphasizes the ability to play effectively on the entire rink.

HOCKEY FACTS

There are eight classifications of ice hockey in Great Britain:

under 10 years
under 12 years
under 14 years
under 16 years
under 19 years
seniors
women (mixed hockey is permitted up to the 16-year age group)
recreational

Glossary

assist The pass to the player who scores a goal.

backhand pass Passing to a team-mate who is behind the player

body-check Using the body legally to move an opposing player away from the puck by moving a shoulder or hip into that player

centre The offensive player in the middle who is responsible for setting up offensive plays

clearing Moving the puck far away from any players; generally a defensive technique

cross-checking Using a stick to check a player across the body above the waist; a foul

crossover A skating manoeuvre made by placing one skate over the other to change direction or increase speed

digging Pushing out the puck from an opponent or along the side boards

drop pass A passing manoeuvre in which a player simply leaves the puck behind so a team-mate can get it

face-off The referee drops the puck fairly between two players to start play

forechecking An action by the offensive players to get the puck away from the other team in their defensive zone

goalie The position responsible for guarding the net: the goalie has heavier padding than other players and uses a larger stick and a glove to stop and catch the puck

hooking Using a stick to grab a player around the arm or leg to slow or stop a play; a foul

icing Shooting the puck over three lines to stop offensive pressure; icing causes a face-off in the defensive zone of the team that committed the error

offside When any player gets into the offensive zone before the puck

penalty minutes The amount of time a player spends off the ice because of a penalty

playing short-handed When a team plays with four or fewer players because fouls have sent those players off the ice

power play When one team has more players on the ice because of fouls, it has more 'power' to score a goal

puck The one-inch by three-inch (2.5 cm by 7.5 cm) hard, circular piece of rubber that is the centre of the game; a puck is frozen solid before game time so it won't bounce on the ice

shift A period of time spent playing; a player can play several shifts in one game

Stanley Cup The trophy that represents the championship of the National Hockey League

stick Wood, fibreglass, or aluminium shaft, with a blade, that is used to move the puck

tip-in Using the blade of a stick to deflect the puck and change its direction toward and into the goal

Vezina Trophy The award given to the National Hockey League goalie who allows in the fewest goals per game in a season

wings Offensive players who play on the far left and right sides of the rink

zone coverage A defensive set-up of players that requires each player to cover a particular area and prevent offensive players from attacking

Index